Usborne
First Sticker Book
Under the Sea

Illustrated by Cecilia Johansson

Contents

There are lots of stickers at the back
of this book for you to stick on each page.

Designed by Stephanie Jones

Words by Jessica Greenwell

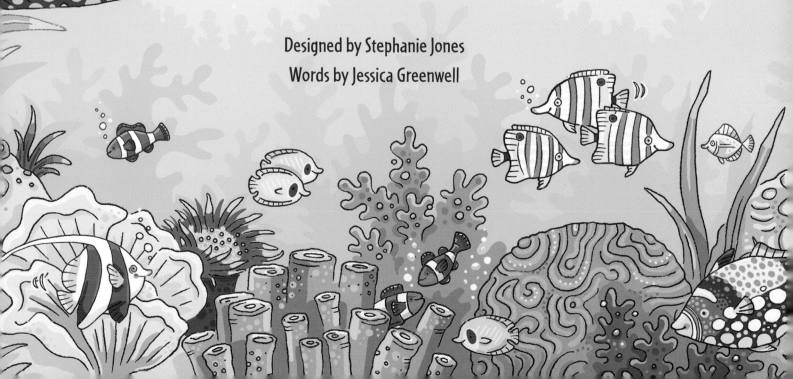

Coral reef

All kinds of different fish swim around coral reefs.
Add some butterfly fish to the picture.

Freezing waters

In the Antarctic the sea is cold and icy.
Put humpback whales and penguins in the water.

Playful dolphins

Dolphins love to splash and play. Can you
put a mother dolphin and her baby in the sea?

Underwater forest

Kelp forests are full of giant sea plants.
Add a shark and some jellyfish to the picture.

Snow and ice

It's snowy and cold in the Arctic. Find a place
for walruses and swimming seals.

By the seashore

The water is warm and clear in this pool by the seashore.
Where could you put some crabs and starfish?

The shipwreck

This old ship has sunk to the bottom of the sea.
Can you find a place for some divers looking for treasure?

On the seabed

Lots of animals live at the bottom of the sea.
Stick some flatfish and lobsters on the sand.

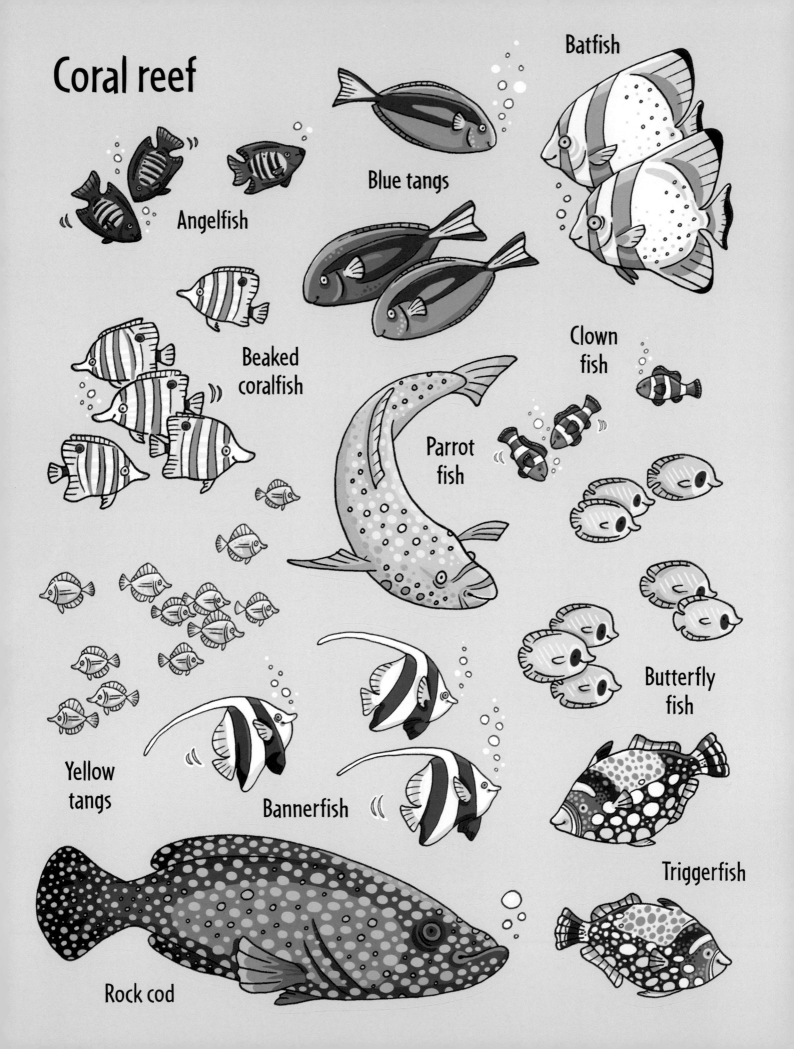

Coral reef

Batfish

Blue tangs

Angelfish

Beaked
coralfish

Clown
fish

Parrot
fish

Butterfly
fish

Yellow
tangs

Bannerfish

Triggerfish

Rock cod

Freezing waters

Emperor penguins

Humpback whales

Adélie penguins

Playful dolphins

Mackerel

Bottlenose
dolphins

Underwater forest

Sea otters

Leopard shark

Sea lions

Jellyfish

Garibaldi fish

Sunfish

Snow and ice

Narwhals

Squid

Ringed seals

Walruses

Orca (killer whale)

Arctic cod

By the seashore

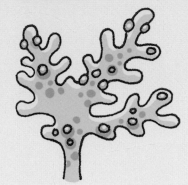

Seaweed

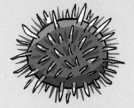

Sea urchins

Starfish

Sea snails

Hermit crabs

Sea anemones

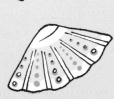

Limpets

Mussels

Blennies

The shipwreck

Green turtles

Divers

Hammerhead
sharks

Zebra fish

Reef sharks

Manta ray

On the seabed

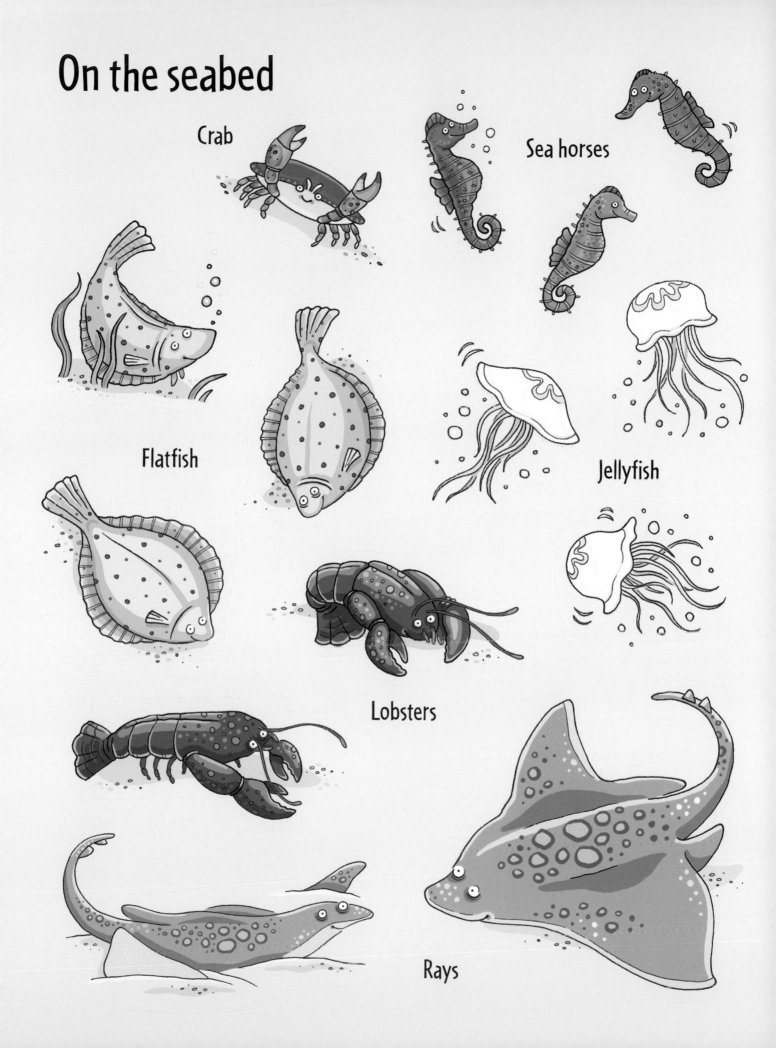

Crab

Sea horses

Flatfish

Jellyfish

Lobsters

Rays